REGIONS OF THE U.S.A.

The West

by Rebecca Felix

PUBLISHED BY THE CHILD'S WORLD ®

The Child's World

Published by The Child's World®
1980 Lookout Drive • Mankato, MN 56003-1705
800-599-READ • www.childsworld.com

Acknowledgments
The Child's World®: Mary Berendes, Publishing Director
Red Line Editorial: Editorial direction
The Design Lab: Design
Amnet: Production
Design Element: Dreamstime

Photographs ©: iStockphoto/Thinkstock, title, 10, 11, 16, 24, 25;
Photodisc, title, 21; Brand X Images, title, 27; Creatas, 3; Comstock/
Thinkstock, 3; Digital Vision/Thinkstock, 3; Mariusz S. Jurgielewicz/
Shutterstock Images, 4; Red Line Editorial, Inc., 5, 6; Richard A. McMillin/
Shutterstock Images, 7; Konrad Mostert/Shutterstock Images, 8, 31;
Shutterstock Images, 9, 14, 15, 19, 20, 26, 28; Library of Congress, 12,
13; Patrick Poendl/Shutterstock Images, 17; Dudarev Mikhail/Shutterstock
Images, 18; Andrew Zarivny/Shutterstock Images, 22; Gary Paul Lewis/
Shutterstock Images, 23; Byron W. Moore/Shutterstock Images, 29

Front cover: iStockphoto/Thinkstock; Creatas; Photodisc; Comstock/
Thinkstock; Brand X Pictures; Digital Vision/Thinkstock

ISBN: 978-1623234959
LCCN: 2013931429

Printed in the United States of America
Mankato, MN
July, 2013
PA02170

ABOUT THE AUTHOR

Rebecca Felix is a writer and editor who grew up in the Midwest. She received a bachelor's degree in English from the University of Minnesota, which is her home state. She has edited and written several children's books and currently lives in Florida, which is in the Southeastern region of the United States.

Table of Contents

CHAPTER ONE

Rockies, Rugged Coast, and Rain

Prairies create wide fields of grass. Mountains stand miles high. Ancient trees as tall as skyscrapers grow near the rocky coast. This region of the United States is the West. Eleven states with different landscapes make up the West. These states are divided into subregions by geography.

Geography

The eastern halves of Colorado, Montana, and Wyoming are in the Great Plains. The land here is mainly flat. The western parts

Part of the West sits on the Pacific Ocean coast.

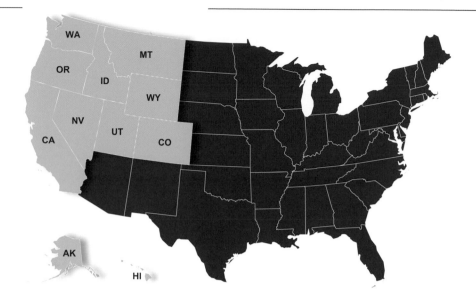

of these states are covered by the Rocky Mountains. This is the largest range in North America. It has a very high elevation. Many of its peaks have snow year-round.

Northwest of the Rockies are the Pacific Northwest states. These states include western Idaho, Washington, and Oregon. Eastern Idaho is in the Rocky Mountains. The Pacific Northwest includes mountains, rivers, rocky coasts, and forests. It also includes North America's only rain forest, located in Washington. The rain forest floor is thick with ferns and other plants. The area has many waterfalls, too.

Geography in northern California is similar to the Pacific Northwest. California is home to two very unique types of trees. Redwood trees are the tallest trees in the world. Redwoods grow as tall as skyscrapers. Huge sequoia trees also grow in this area. They grow as tall as redwoods, but their trunks can grow wider.

The California coast also has many beaches. Moving farther south through the state, the landscape turns to desert. The desert also crosses into Nevada and covers most

Redwoods can grow approximately 350 feet (107 m) tall. That is as tall as a building with 35 floors! A sequoia tree trunk can grow 40 feet (12 m) wide. That is the length of a school bus!

Some of Alaska is north of the Arctic Circle. These places sometimes have no sun in winter. And in summer, there is sometimes sun 24 hours a day!

of the state. Utah borders Nevada to the east. Much of its land is desert, mountain, and rocky plateau.

The last two states in the West are Alaska and Hawaii. These are the only two U.S. states not bordering other states. Alaska borders Canada above Washington. Half of Alaska is tundra, frozen ground with no trees. There are also mountains and coast in Alaska. Hawaii is a group of islands in the Pacific Ocean. Volcanoes cover many islands, and beaches make up the coasts.

Climate

The West reaches across many landscapes, which means the climates vary greatly. Hawaii is warm and tropical all year. Average weather in Alaska ranges from cool summers to very cold winters. The Pacific Northwest receives a lot of rain. The Mojave Desert in southern California, Utah, and

Alaska has a much different landscape than the rest of the West.

Nevada gets very little rainfall. Colorado, Idaho, Montana, and Wyoming experience all four seasons.

The climates and landforms in the West lead to extreme weather and events. Hawaii, California, Oregon, and Washington sometimes have volcanic eruptions. These can cause **landslides**. The southern and eastern areas of the West have **droughts**. Droughts can lead to wildfires. All states in the West except Colorado have felt earthquakes.

Wildlife

Alaska is home to black bears, brown bears, and polar bears. Herds of elk live in the Pacific Northwest. Sea turtles and humpback whales swim the waters of Hawaii. Sea lions live along the Pacific Ocean coast. Many types of sharks and fish also swim off the coast. Mountain lions live across California, Nevada, and Utah. Many types

Humpback whales are commonly seen near Hawaii.

CAPITALS OF THE WEST

The only way to Alaska's capital, Juneau, is by boat or plane. It does not have any roads connecting it to the rest of Alaska! Olympia, Washington, has remained the state capital since 1889. It was the territory's capital before that. Salem, Oregon, lies on the Willamette River. Boise, Idaho, is on the Boise River. Helena, Montana, was named after a miner's hometown in Minnesota. Cheyenne, Wyoming, was named after the Cheyenne Native Americans from the area. Denver, Colorado, is called Mile High City because its elevation is one mile above sea level. Salt Lake City, Utah, lies on the Great Salt Lake. This lake is so salty fish cannot live in it. Carson City, Nevada, was a part of the Utah territory before the Nevada territory was established. Sacramento, California, is famous for being a gold rush town. Honolulu, Hawaii, is on the island of Oahu.

of lizards and snakes live in the Nevada desert. The Great Plains are home to herds of buffalo.

CHAPTER TWO

Growth, Gold, and Railroad

Eskimo people still live in Alaska today.

The first people in North America were the Paleo-Indians. They are the ancestors of Native American people. Native Americans formed many tribes and moved across the continent. Tribes in the West included Nez Perce, Chinook, Cheyenne, Blackfoot, Arapaho, and Ute. The first people of Hawaii were from French Polynesia. Paleo-Aleut people also came to North America. They are the ancestors of the Aleut people in Alaska. Eskimos are native people of Alaska as well.

The Louisiana Purchase cost $15 million. Interest turned the actual price into more than $27 million.

The eastern colonies gained independence from Great Britain in the late 1700s. The colonies became the United States. Explorers started moving west.

France controlled some land west of the Mississippi River. The United States bought this land from France in 1803. This was called the Louisiana Purchase. The land included parts of Colorado, Wyoming, and Montana. Explorers Meriwether Lewis and William Clark traveled the new territory. They saw many new animals and landscapes.

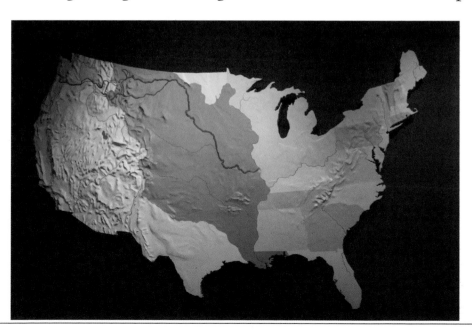

The Louisiana Purchase included land from the West.

People began moving west after Lewis and Clark's journey. The path through the West was busy with travelers through the 1840s. This path is known as the Oregon Trail. Many Native Americans were pushed off their land as settlers moved in.

Other countries still controlled land in southern parts of the West. This led to the Mexican-American War from 1846 to 1848. The United States gained parts of Colorado, California, Nevada, and Utah after the war. The United States also gained land from Great Britain in the late 1840s. That land became Oregon, Washington, and Idaho.

Gold was discovered in California in 1848. Thousands of people rushed West hoping to find gold and get rich. This is known as the California Gold Rush.

Levi Strauss traveled to California during the gold rush. He made pants for miners. These pants became known as jeans. The Levi brand is still popular today.

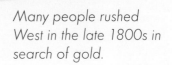

Many people rushed West in the late 1800s in search of gold.

The railroad greatly shortened travel time. Before the railroad, it could take two to six months to travel 2,000 miles (3,200 km). By train it took approximately six days.

The United States began building a major railroad system in the late 1800s. It connected the east and the west. The Transcontinental Railroad brought many more people West. People building the railroad hunted bison for food and trade. Bison almost became **extinct**. Many people relied on bison to survive. Railroad construction also **displaced** Native Americans. These things led to battles between the United States and Native Americans. The Battle of the Little Bighorn in Montana was one. Native Americans won that battle, but they were pushed off their land.

There are many stories of the battles and events of the early West. These stories made it seem like a wild place. It became known as the Wild West.

Pearl Harbor is a popular tourist destination today.

Settlers moved to Alaska in the late 1800s and early 1900s. Many were looking for gold. Alaska became a U.S. state in 1959. Hawaii was a U.S. territory in the 1940s. An attack at Pearl Harbor, Hawaii, in 1941 brought the United States into World War II (1939–1945). Hawaii became a U.S. state in 1959.

Present Day

Throughout history, the West was a place of mystery and adventure. Some people still think of it this way. The West

THE WILD WEST

The Wild West was a place of adventure in the 1800s. Its open lands represented opportunity. But stories of the West also involved danger and mystery. Wild West stories included shootouts, saloons, and rowdy behavior. The people who settled the area were depicted as rough and tough. Stories about Native Americans being wild were common, too. Some tales of the Wild West were made up, but some were true. The huge canyons, hot springs, and mountains from the stories were real. The Wild West was the subject of many books and movies. Stories of how the West was tamed are still popular today.

was the last region of the United States to be settled. Its history is still very new. And the influences of its first cultures are still present today.

CHAPTER THREE

Tolerance, Technology, and Tourism

California's government is working hard to pass many environmental laws.

Each state in the West has three branches of government. These are the executive, legislative, and judicial branches. The head of the executive branch is the governor. Governors manage state programs, policies, and laws.

The legislative branch keeps a state budget on track. It also

Wind farms are becoming more popular in California as part of the green movement.

Hawaii is also a green state. It banned plastic shopping bags statewide in 2012.

creates state laws. Laws can be different from state to state. Some issues are more important to one state than to another. West Coast states are known to be green. Being green means caring about and protecting the environment. California has been a leader of the green movement for many years. It recently passed many environmental laws. One gives businesses **tax credits** if they use green energy.

The judicial branch is a state's court system. Court systems are also broken into county and city courts.

Local governments manage police and fire departments. They also take care of parks. Governments own many parks.

The government owns half of the land in Wyoming and California. The land includes parks and forestland.

Economy

Commercial fishing is important to the **economy** in Alaska and West Coast states. Commercial fishing means catching fish to make money. This includes ocean and river fishing. Salmon has been a major **export** in the West throughout history.

Washington has a successful agriculture **industry**. It is one of the top three U.S. states for farming exports. Apples and cherries are exported from Washington. The timber industry is also

More than half of U.S. seafood caught through commercial fishing is from Alaska.

Salmon is one of the biggest exports in the West.

important in Washington. Producing wood products is a major part of Oregon's economy. Electronics have also become a major export in Oregon.

California has a very successful technology industry. It is home to Silicon Valley. This is the technology center of the nation. Many computer products are made here. Several large technology businesses are located here. California has many other large and successful industries. These include agriculture, clean energy, and tourism.

California is the world's largest seller of almonds. It has the perfect climate and growing conditions.

Timber is a large industry in Washington.

Las Vegas, Nevada, is a popular tourist destination.

Tourism is also big in Nevada's major cities, Reno and Las Vegas. Many tourists visit these cities to **gamble** in the many casinos. Gold and copper are two of Nevada's exports. Utah's important industries are mining and tourism. Coal is a top export in Wyoming. A little less than half of the nation's coal is produced here.

Approximately 50 million tourists visit the Pacific Coast every year.

TOURING THE WEST

Tourism brings money and jobs to the West. Redwood National Park and Sequoia National Park are in California. They are home to ancient, giant trees. Yosemite National Park is in California, too. It has tall mountains and waterfalls. California beaches also attract many visitors. Olympic National Park is in Washington. People travel here to see its mountains and rain forest. Wyoming and Montana landscapes attract hunting and fishing tourists. The Colorado Rockies draw many skiers. City tourism is also big in the West. Los Angeles, California, is a center of entertainment. Many famous musicians and movie stars live there. The city has many restaurants, theaters, and hotels.

Some of Colorado's main exports are meat and electronics. Having fun and being active is more important to Montana's economy. Popular activities in Montana include hunting, skiing, and fishing.

CHAPTER FOUR

Hollywood, Healthy Food, and Hiking

Hollywood, California, is home to the film industry.

People who settled the West came from around the world. This was because of the California Gold Rush. People of many cultures still live in the West today. This region is home to many **ethnicities**. It also has a large population.

More than 75 percent of Californians live in one of three cities: Los Angeles, San Francisco, and San Diego.

The population of California lives mainly in large cities. Major cities include Los Angeles, San Diego, and San Francisco. Many people in California work in show business. This is because Hollywood is in Los Angeles. It is the center of the film industry. California is also where many types of music were created, including West Coast jazz and West Coast hip hop. People on the West Coast are much like people across the U.S. They participate in many activities.

Surfing is another popular activity on the West Coast.

Swimming, yoga, hiking, biking, and other outdoor activities are popular.

There are some misunderstandings about the West. One is that Washington is always rainy. This is not true. The area does get a lot of rain, but its summers tend to be mild and sunny.

Alaska has fewer people per square mile than any other state in the West. The number of people living within one square mile (2.6 sq km) is called the population density. Montana and Wyoming also have low population densities.

Many Mormons live in Utah, but not everyone in Utah is Mormon.

Mormons are a certain type of Christians. Salt Lake City, Utah, is a center of the Mormon religion, and many Mormons live there. However, Utah is home to people of many religions, just like the rest of the West.

Montana has seven Native American reservations.

Organic and vegetarian dishes are popular in the West.

Most Alaskans speak English. But many also speak one or more of the 21 native Alaskan languages.

Food

The ethnic diversity of the West Coast influences its food. Nearly all types of cuisine can be found here. This includes Hispanic and Asian foods. Many people on the West Coast are healthy eaters. They care about eating fresh foods. Organic or vegetarian dishes are common. Seafood is also a major part of West Coast diets. This is because of the region's location on the Pacific Ocean. A Japanese cuisine called Sushi is popular. Rice and raw fish are its main ingredients. Sushi dishes are served cold.

Foods in Southern California and Nevada are similar to food in the Southwest. Native American and Hispanic

cultures influence the foods. Dishes often include corn, chiles, tomatoes, and beans. Many dishes are served in tortillas.

The people who first settled the West also influenced foods of the Great Plains and Rocky Mountain area. Hunting was important to early settlers in the West. Dishes often include venison, bison, and deer. Beef and steak are also popular. The many types of foods and many peoples of the West make it a region unlike any other.

Hawaiian is a native language of Hawaii. It is an official state language along with English.

Dishes in the West include meat, like venison. This was influenced by early settlers.

RECIPE

CALIFORNIA ROLL

Ingredients:

1 package pre-made sushi rice

Pre-sliced cucumbers

1 package imitation crabmeat

1 can avocado

1 sheet dried seaweed

bamboo mat

plastic wrap

Directions:

Cut 3–4 cucumber slices into little strips. Dice 2–3 pieces of imitation crabmeat into small cubes. Cut a few pieces of avocado. Set all three ingredients aside. Place a layer of plastic wrap on the bamboo mat. Place the dried seaweed on top of the plastic wrap. Make sure the shiny side is facing down. Cover the top side of the dried seaweed with water. Grab a handful of the rice and spread across the dried seaweed. Place the cucumber, avocado, and crabmeat in the center of the rice. Spread ingredients to form a long line. Pick up a short side of the bamboo mat. Roll everything into a cylinder. Remove the bamboo mat and plastic wrap. Cut into slices and enjoy!

Fast Facts

Population: 64,940,638 (2012 estimate)

Most populous state: California (38,041,430, 2012 estimate)

Least populous state: Wyoming (576,412, 2012 estimate)

Area: 1,516,161 square miles (3,926,839 sq km)

Highest temperature: 134 degrees Fahrenheit (57°C) in California in 1913

Lowest temperature: minus-80 degrees Fahrenheit (-62°C) in Alaska in 1971

Largest cities: Los Angeles, California; San Diego, California; San Jose, California; San Francisco, California; Seattle, Washington; Denver, Colorado; Portland, Oregon

Major sports teams: Denver Broncos (NFL, football); Los Angeles Lakers (NBA, basketball): Oakland A's (MLB, baseball); San Diego Chargers (NFL, football); San Francisco 49ers (NFL, football); San Francisco Giants (MLB, baseball); Seattle Seahawks (NFL, football)

Glossary

displaced (dis-PLASED) People are displaced when they are moved from their usual place. Native Americans in the West were displaced when a railroad was built.

droughts (drouts) Droughts are long periods of time without rain. The Great Plains states in the West experience droughts.

economy (i-KON-uh-mee) Economy is the system of making, buying, and selling things. Seafood is important to the economy in the West.

ethnicities (eth-NIH-sit-ees) Ethnicities are associations with certain groups of people of the same culture. People of many ethnicities settled the West.

export (EK-sport) An export is a product made in one place and sold to another place. Salmon is a major export of Alaska.

extinct (ek-STINGKT) Something is extinct when it no longer exists anywhere. Bison were hunted so much on the Great Plains they almost became extinct.

gamble (GAM-buhl) To gamble is to make a bet or play a game of chance to try to win money. Many people visit Las Vegas to gamble in the casinos.

industry (IN-duh-stree) An industry is a group of businesses. The center of the nation's technology industry is in Silicon Valley, California.

landslides (LAND-slides) Landslides are when great amounts of earth, rock, or mud rush downward. Earthquakes can cause landslides.

tax credits (TAKS KRED-its) Tax credits are money a person or business can subtract from what they pay to a government each year. California offers tax credits if businesses use green energy.

Learn More

Books

Rau, Dana Meachen. *The West*. New York: Scholastic, 2012.

Stone, Tanya Lee. *Regional Wild America: Unique Animals of the Mountains and Prairies*. Detroit, MI: Blackbirch Press, 2005.

Walker, Robert. *What's in the West?* New York: Crabtree Publishing Company, 2011.

Web Sites

Visit our Web site for links about the West:

childsworld.com/links

Note to Parents, Teachers, and Librarians: We routinely verify our Web links to make sure they are safe and active sites. So encourage your readers to check them out!

Index